Didjeridu Dreaming

Adrian Parker

 J.B. BOOKS AUSTRALIA

DIDJERIDU DREAMING
Published in 2003 by
J.B. Books Pty Ltd
PO Box 118, Marleston South Australia 5033
PH: (08) 8351 1688

ISBN 1 876622 43 1

Design: Robert Moller
Production: Victoria Jefferys, WriteLight Pty Ltd
Printed in China through Phoenix Offset.

Contents

The Didjeridu

The didjeridu is one of the most popular and dynamic instruments throughout Australia and the world. Its rich and vibrant sound mystifies and enchants those who hear it, and entices many young people to learn to play. Once mastered, the didjeridu becomes a source of inspiration, creativity, relaxation and meditation. People can teach themselves to play and it does not require an ability to read music.

Its history can be traced from the present day back through time with ochre paintings rendered on ancient rock faces.

This book presents an informative overview of the manufacture, history, mythology and role of the didjeridu in Aboriginal society. It also contains lessons and exercises on how to play the didjeridu. Breathing techniques, sound and rhythm are all discussed.

The didjeridu is a wind instrument that has been manufactured and played by Aboriginal Australians since time immemorial. It is primarily a hollow log or length of bamboo, with a wax mouthpiece attached to one end. A didjeridu is usually one to two metres in length.

The hollow in wooden didjeridus is created by termites; small light intolerant ant-like insects that harvest and eat grass and timber. They live in individual colonies or nests containing a queen who oversees and produces thousands of workers.

When playing a didjeridu the musician blows into one end using loosely pursed lips. If the vibration of his lips matches the

**A selection of Arnhem Land didjeridus.
From right to left :
(1) antique didjeridu, (2) made by Chris
Ngaboy, (3) Chris Ngaboy, (4) Chris Ngaboy,
(5) Alex Nganjmirra, (6) Joshua Bangar.**

resonance frequency of the instrument, it will cause it to vibrate and increase in volume. This creates the characteristic drone for which the didjeridu is famous. Circular breathing allows the musician to create a continuous sound.

Early explorers named the instrument 'didjeridu', a term based on its sound. During the first century of European settlement there was only occasional reference made to the didjeridu, usually by explorers scribbling notes in journals.

An explosion of public interest pertaining to primitive cultures took place during the late 18th and early 19th centuries. Increasing numbers of anthropologists and adventure writers visited Australian shores recording and publishing their experiences.

Today the didjeridu has gained international prominence and is played and enjoyed by people throughout the world. It has been promoted and encouraged by proponents like Rolf Harris, Charlie McMahon and Yothu Yindi. They have brought the sounds of the didjeridu into people's homes and living rooms.

Antiquity

Over the years there has been great debate about the age of the didjeridu. Some speculative estimates have placed it as being up to 10,000 years of age, however the didjeridu's origins can be found in more recent times.

In tropical Australia, timber and fibre products, particularly bamboo, if left exposed to the elements decompose quickly from moisture, humidity, animals and insects — notably, termites. This has made it difficult for archaeo-logical digs to ascertain the antiquity of the didjeridu — they have much greater success in the analysis of stone tools and artefacts.

One of the most insightful ways of estimating didjeridu antiquity is by the analysis of rock paintings in which they are depicted and determining their approximate age. Ecological and environmental conditions help give further insight.

Australia's ecological pre-history consisted of several phases — the Pre-Estuarine, Estuarine and Freshwater Periods. These periods correlate with the rock art styles that have existed over the millennia.

During the Pre-Estuarine period widespread glaciation created lower sea levels resulting in the Kakadu — Arnhem Land region being further inland and more desolate than today. The coast was situated approximately 400 kilometres further north.

Gradual global warming brought the Pre-Estuarine period to an end about 8,000 years ago — the beginning of the Estuarine Period. Rising seas gradually made the area more coastal and fertile.

Habitats have evolved in response to these dramatic climatic and environmental changes. Accordingly, the familiar coastal, floodplain and woodland environments of today have existed for the last three thousand years — the Freshwater Period.

During this time stable sea levels have allowed the formation of vast freshwater flood plains and river deltas, encouraging growth of wetland and woodland habitats. These habitats contain the bamboos and hardwoods necessary for the manufacture of didjeridus. It is during the freshwater period that the didjeridu probably first originated.[1,2]

Rock paintings from the era contain depictions of the didjeridu being played in corroborees and ceremonies. Hook headed and simple stick figure painting styles appear to dominate paintings of people associated with the instrument. Like many artefacts, the didjeridu does not appear to be included in paintings of earlier styles and phases. One bi-chromal painting of a figure in headdress playing the didjeridu located at Mount Borradaile in Western Arnhem Land was probably rendered in the latter part of the Freshwater Period.

1. Rock Art of the Dreamtime, J. Flood, p. 261-2. 2. Journey in Time, G. Chaloupka, p. 89.

Bamboo was the favoured material for making didjeridus as it is softer than hardwood and easier to cut with stone tools. About three hundred years ago Macassan fishermen from Indonesia started harvesting trepang (sea slug or beech-de-meer) along the north Australian coast. Among the variety of tools, diseases and language, they introduced the steel axe and hatchet. These tools allowed hardwood didjeridus to be cut and manufactured with greater ease. Today, timber didjeridus are preferable to their bamboo counterparts.

Steel tools introduced by Macassans, and later, Europeans, revolutionised didjeridu manufacture. Location: Hawk Dreaming, Kakadu National Park.

Alice Moyle (in World Archaeology) notes that bamboo and timber didjeridus can be distinguished in some rock paintings by the way they are decorated. Bamboo instruments may have the nodes featured, while didjeridus decorated with linear designs may be made from timber.

A stick figure painting of a man playing a didjeridu held aloft. To the left of him is a figure playing music sticks. The stick figures to the right could be dancers in accompaniment. Location: Hawk Dreaming, Kakadu National Park

A seated hook headed figure wearing elbow tassels playing a flared and decorated 'mole'. Behind him is a spear thrower and spears. On the left is another seated figure with hands placed on knees. Location: Hawk Dreaming, Kakadu National Park

Two seated figures in the cross-legged position. The figure on the right is playing a didjeridu held aloft. Behind him is a spear thrower and spears. The figure to the left is playing music sticks. Location: Hawk Dreaming, Kakadu National Park.

A seated hook headed figure with elbow tassels, playing a raised didjeridu. Kneeling to the right is another figure playing music sticks. Location: Hawk Dreaming, Kakadu National Park.

A standing figure, wearing headdress, playing the didjeridu. This painting is bi-chromal, containing red and yellow ochre. Location: Mount Borradaile, Western Arnhem Land.

'Making music' by Alex Nganjmirra. Painted on paper, this contemporary picture of a corroboree closely resembles its predecessors on rock faces.

Early accounts

Early European accounts of the didjeridu were made in conjunction with observations of Aboriginal life and culture, primarily corroborees and dance. References to it were fleeting, concentrating on the context in which the instrument was used, rather than techniques used to play it.

Some of the first observations of the didjeridu were made by people stationed with the British Garrison at Raffles Bay on the Coburg Peninsula in northwest Arnhem Land. It was described as 'being of bamboo and about three feet long.' A drawing of an Aboriginal man playing the instrument at Raffles Bay appeared in T.B. Wilson's *Narrative of a Voyage Round the World* in 1835. (Moyle, p. 322.)

Around 1846 John Sweatman noted...

> *'They have a kind of musical instrument made of a bamboo pipe about three feet long and from one to two inches in diameter from which they draw a succession of monotonous but not disagreeable notes...'*

(Allen and Corris 1977.)

In 1893 R Etheridge Jr. wrote that didjeridus...

> *'are made from bamboo lengths, the diaphragms having been removed, probably by dropping live coals down the tubes....Judging by the size, therefore, the trumpets are probably made of B. arnhemica. They are all about the same length and appear to be very difficult for the uninitiated to blow...'*

(The Australian Didgeridu in World Archaeology Vol 12, Moyle, p. 322)

Half a century later this description, originally accompanied by a photograph, was made by Charles Percy Mountford during his Grand Scientific Expedition to Oenpelli in 1948. Mountford also made some of the first tape recordings of the didjeridu...

> *'An Aboriginal Gabriel Blows a Primitive Trumpet: the Men Jump to the Rhythm. A most important part of the orchestra, he puffs ceaselessly into the long drone tube, a didgeridoo.'...*

(National Geographic, p.768-9.)

The radio journalist Colin Simpson made a much more informative observation...

> *'Now the didjeridu-man has come in, and he sits down beside the song man. He stretches out one thin black leg and spreads his big toe wide from his other toes. The end of the didgeridoo projects just beyond the end of his rested foot and is about two and a half inches across, bigger than the other end, which he raises to his mouth. The didjeridu is wet, he has poured water down the hollow wooden tube to give it better tone. About a quarter of its length is painted red-black-red-black in narrow rings, the rest is unpainted wood, smooth from its use in many hands...*
>
> *The didjeridu mans lips are lost in his instrument, his cheeks and his chest rise and fall. The vibrant drone of the didjeridu winds out and through the songman's chant...'*

(Adam in Ochre, Simpson, p.11-12)

Aboriginal Society and the Didjeridu

The didjeridu is unique to Aborigines from the northern aspects of Australia, generally, above the Tropic of Capricorn. It originated in coastal areas near the Arnhem Land plateau in the Northern Territory, its use spreading to the Kimberly and Pilbara in Western Australia and Queenslands Cape York peninsula in more recent times.[1] It was not commonly used in the central desert regions or the southern and eastern aspects of the continent. People in these areas have their own unique cultures and customs.

Interestingly, areas where Aborigines traditionally used the didjeridu correlate closely with the distribution of stringybark *(Eucalyptus tetrodonta)* and woollybutt *(Eucalyptus miniata)*.[2]

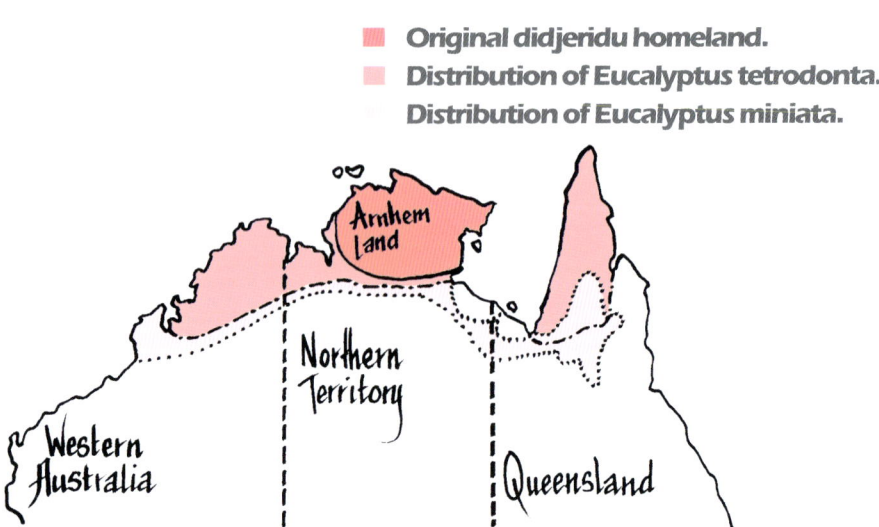

■ **Original didjeridu homeland.**
■ **Distribution of Eucalyptus tetrodonta.**
■ **Distribution of Eucalyptus miniata.**

1. Journey in Time, G. Chaloupka, p. 89.
2. Didjeridu — A Complete Guide, J. Bowden, p. 9.

The didjeridu plays an important role in the social and spiritual life of Aboriginal people. In the absence of writing, stories and knowledge were handed orally from generation to generation. Art, music and song were important mediums of communication and were used in conjunction with oral teachings. Group participation was common, creating a sense of unity and community among performers and observers.

The didjeridu is rarely played solo. Accompaniment includes music sticks, voice, hand clapping, bark and buttock slapping. Often the didjeridu player will play music sticks or tap his instrument with a single music stick or finger. The instrument is used for entertainment, corroborees (in which the entire community participate) and highly secret and sacred men's ceremonies. These include the Lorrkon (mortuary), Kunapipi and Ubar ceremonies in Western Arnhem Land. Sacred didjeridus were often stored in a secret location and used for ceremony only. At the completion of the ceremony they were returned to their hiding place.

The story of Ubar is based on the exploits of Yirrbardbard, his wife and mother-in-law. Yirrbardbard's wife had been refusing to sleep with him and her mother condoned her action. This made Yirrbardbard very angry and he decided to kill them. One day when he saw the two women approaching a hollow log he turned into a snake and slid into the log, scratching the inside so the women would think it was a snake or bandicoot. The women, thinking dinner was at hand, knelt at each end inserting a hand into the log in order to catch their prey. Yirrbardbard bit and killed both women. Fearing payback Yirrbardbard was advised by a kangaroo, Nadulmi, that a ceremony honouring the women could avoid this. (Kunwinjku Art, p. 80.)

Ubar ceremony involves the use of didjeridu accompanied by the Balnooknook (Ubar) drum, which is made from a section of hollow tree …

'The balnooknook-man is rising with the drum. Now, led by the didjeridu-man, who plays a long note on the didjeridu as he comes, the men rush forward with the balnooknook. They place the drum between the two initiates who have knelt down, the length of the balnooknook apart. The nakumdoit place their hands in the hollow ends of the drum. Each uncle takes his boy's head between his palms and sways it from side to side. The songman bends over the initiates, all the men bend over them, and, loudly and fervently, the two youths are "sung" to the accompaniment of the didjeridu.'

(Adam in Ochre, Simpson, p.13.)

In Kunapipi ceremony the sound of the didjeridu represents the voice of a mythical snake...

'To produce these sounds, the initiated performer 'has to lie down to play the instrument which is rested in a horizontal position on two low supports just off the ground'

(The Australian Didgeridu in World Archaeology, vol 12, Moyle, p.327.)

Throughout Northern Australia the didjeridu has many different names, reflecting the diversity of tribal and language groups. It is called *yidaki* in eastern Arnhem Land, and *mole*, in Western Arnhem Land. Early European visitors to Coburg Peninsula noted that local Aborigines used the word *eboro*, while inhabitants of Groote Eylandt call it *yiraga*. In the Kimberly the term for didjeridu is *ganbag*.

George Chaloupka writes that...

'In the past the didjeridu was made from a length of angole, the bamboo (Bambusa arnhemica), from which the name mole is derived.'

(Journey in Time, Chaloupka, p 189.)

It is believed that if a woman does play, she will become pregnant, and possibly develop facial hair.

Women take part in corrobories where the didjeridu is used, often singing, tapping music sticks and dancing in accompaniment. Not all men play, as like any instrument, some master it better than others, though most will have a go in informal surrounds. Men also have specialist roles in society, ceremonial and spiritual life. Some are designated as didjeridu players, song men, dancers or artists during dance and ceremony.

One commonly held misnomer is that non-Aboriginal women should not play the didjeridu — that it is taboo to all women. The inhabitants of the Kakadu and Western Arnhem Land, the region where the instrument originated, maintain that it is perfectly O.K. for Western women to play…

'It's a Culture thing, Balanda daluk (white women) are not Binninj (Aboriginal). They can play. Different culture…'

Interview, Alex Nganjmirra, 1996.

Stories explaining the origin of the instrument vary regionally and come in numerous forms. Some are quite romantic, others disturbing. Some stories maintain that the didjeridu was discovered when wind blew on a hollow log, while others involve people blowing into them. This story is from Cape York…

> *'In the beginning, all was cold and dark. Burbuk Boon was preparing wood for the fire, to bring warmth and light, to protect his family. Burbook Boon added more wood to the fire, and as he did he noticed that one of the logs was hollow, and a family of termites was busily feeding on the heartwood in the centre of the log. Not wanting to hurt the termites, Burbook Boon put the hollow log to his mouth and began to blow…*
>
> *The termites flew into the night sky and turned into the stars and the Milky Way, lighting up the land, and for the first time the sound of the didjeridu blessed Mother Earth, protecting her and all Dreamtime spirits with the eternal vibration…'*

Opening dialogue, 'Indiginy- live at the *Rock*', 1994.

This story from Western Arnhem Land, narrated by Alex Nganjmirra is not a Dreamtime story. Alex says it has happened since then and possibly reflecting the relatively recent use of the didjeridu in Aboriginal society. He also says that the story's central character, Bilk Bilk was very short and from another region.

The story makes a strong correlation between men's genitals and the didjeridu. It helps explain why the didjeridu viewed as a men's instrument and symbol of fertility…

'That's Bilk Bilk. You can see that one got the long penis. He went out and used to kill the people. He was bad. So the people they made a little hole to make him go down, to fall in and then kill him. Get a spear. He was bad guy killing and raping. He was an angry man. He used to see a girl, he would rape her.

So the people dug the hole, the parents, you know the mother and father, they got a bit upset and all them uncles, cousins, brothers of them girls, the ones he raped, so they angry at Bilk Bilk as he was raping and killing and they dug the hole and telled him to come here, come here, more better. So he walked toward them but Bilk Bilk couldn't see the hole, it was a trap. They covered them leaves, you know, leaves to make it so he would reckon it was flat ground, but there was a hole covered with leaves.

Bilk Bilk walked toward the people and then he went down, fell down the hole. The people they came back and got spear and threw it, speared him, but he didn't die, he was still alive, so he got his dick and cut it off. Made big didjeridu, that's the one he's holding, didjeridu. That's his dick. He said 'I'm still alive, I'm not killed, still alive', so he made that song.

He made that song for us, for everybody he said sing. He blowed and we made ourselves song, for Kunwinjku people and all other people, everybody. After he played the song he died. The men said we go now because he told us we got to look around and make song for them other people. The people went out and look around them tree, them didjeridu, look around and see if any are hollow and cut it and make a didjeridu. Bilk Bilk taught the people music. Women (Aboriginal) are not allowed to play, only for Binninj man, yeah, them dick, not ladies. The women can dance.'

(Images in Ochre, Parker, p. 85.)

16

The anthropologists Ronald and Catherine Berndt recorded a well-known story at Oenpelli in western Arnhem Land during the late 1940's. It concerns Aranga, the green ant, a malevolent spirit with an abnormally large penis and two lost sisters...

> *Thinking Aranga was human, they consented to sex, which left them sore and bleeding. In retribution, Aboriginal men dug a large pit and lured Aranga into it, where he was beaten, speared and buried. But Aranga survived, and was later heard playing his penis like a didjeridu.'*

(Ancient Ochres, Roberts and Parker.)

Manufacture

Chainsaws, power tools, western paints and brushes have revolution-ised didjeridu making, largely as a response to enormous consumer demand. In Kakadu and western Arnhem Land craftsmen still make the instrument by hand. In contrast to the large numbers produced by commercial manufacturers, a skilled craftsman can produce one didjeridu a day.

Didjeridus are made mostly throughout the first half of the dry season in northern Australia (April-September). This is because following the completion of monsoonal rains, the timber is slowly drying and is relatively easy to cut — if they are made during the wet season, the rain-soaked timber usually splits as it dries. Alternatively, didjeridus are rarely made towards the end of the dry because the timber is too hard to fell with an axe.

Savannah woodlands are easily to accessible during the dry season as flooded creeks and tributaries have subsided. Fire management practises in northern regions mean that flood plains, grasslands and tracts of woodland are burnt every two to three years. Seasonal burning-off removes dense undergrowth in forests, making thoroughfare and navigation easy. This allows craftsmen to obtain suitable tree segments and saplings for didjeridu manufacture.

A large variety of eucalypts are suitable, however stringy bark and woollybutt are preferable, as they are softer and easier to cut than other hard woods. (This also makes them more appealing to varieties of timber eating termite).

Saplings and occasionally tree limbs are selected as potential didjeridus. Craftsmen search for trees displaying features that indicate they may be hollow, as not all trees have termite activity inside them. Upper branches that are dead or dying, hollows, termite trails and nests in or near a tree base signal the possible presence of termites.

To determine if a sapling is hollow the craftsman flicks the trunk with his finger or taps it with a tool. If it makes the correct sound, further investigation is warranted. A small wedge is cut with an axe near the base of the sapling, allowing a visual inspection of the inner trunk to be made. If the hollow is not suitable the tree is left alone and will continue to grow. Termites will often plug the hole to discourage predators and light.

When a suitable sapling is located it is felled, and the length of trunk with which to make an instrument is removed. Saplings contain varying degrees of termite activity, extending partially or all the way up the trunk. Some trees provide only one instrument, others three or four.

The initial rough lengths are called 'blanks'. Once cut, blanks are pounded on the ground to dislodge any termites and dirt that may be inside, making them lighter to carry. They are then transported to the community or camp where the final work is undertaken.

Inspecting a sapling to determine if it will make a suitable didjeridu.

Felling a sapling with a tomahawk.

A hollow stump bearing tell-tale axe marks.

Pounding a blank to remove dirt and unwanted inhabitants.

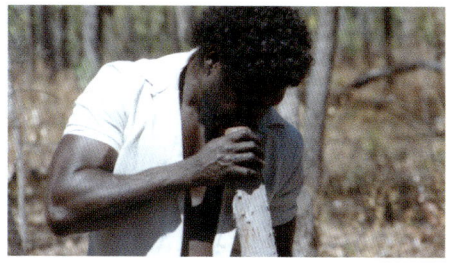

This blank plays nicely- it will make a fine didjeridu.

Which way is the car? Once enough blanks are obtained they are taken back to camp to be transformed into didjeridus.

Back at camp the outer bark is removed from blanks using a machete or hatchet and remaining fibres are cut or scraped away. Internal blockages and remnants of termite dirt are removed by ramming a broomstick or thin pole through the centre of the blank. Water is used to flush out any remaining insects and dirt. The rough ends of the blank are cut away with a handsaw and any small holes along its length filled with bungs or putty. Holes and cracks in didjeridus drastically affect the sound and performance of the instrument.

A rasp file is used to smooth the outer surface of the blank and a rounded mouthpiece is honed at the narrowest end. This makes it comfortable to place to the mouth and play. At last a didjeridu. The entire outer surface is then rubbed with sandpaper to create a smooth finish in preparation for painting, though not all didjeridus are painted.

Rock paintings containing decorated didjeridus indicate that painting the instrument is not a recent practice. The didjeridu makers in Kakadu and Arnhem Land still paint didjeridus with traditional brushes and the four ochre colours — red, white, yellow and black. Ochre occurs naturally, and is most easily found in the vicinity of coastal areas, waterways and washouts. In the past, ochre was an important item of trade.

Didjeridus are painted with techniques similar to those that were used for rock painting. The ochre is ground into a fine powder and mixed with water and a bonding agent, usually P.V.A. glue and applied with bark and reed brushes to the instrument, creating intricate paintings and designs. Typical subjects are human and spirit figures, weapons, flora and fauna, including wallabies and barramundi.

If the wooden mouthpiece of the didjeridu is too rough or wide, the soft dark wax of the native Australian bee (sugarbag) is applied to the timber, and manipulated until satisfactory. A mouthpiece that is too big to be reduced by sugarbag will sometimes have a short section from another hollow log inserted to reduce its diameter.

Stripping the outer bark from a blank.

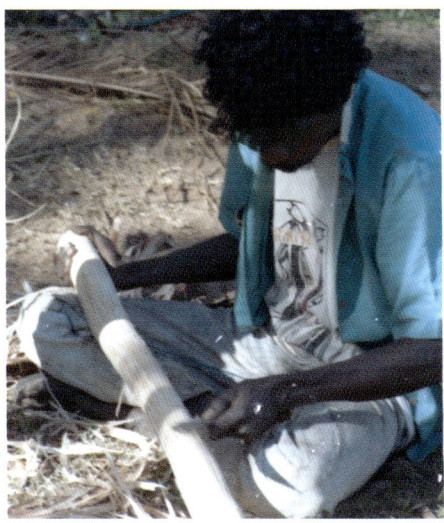

Loose fibres are removed from a blank using a knife.

A pole is used to clear obstructions by ramming it through the hollow centre of the didjeridu.

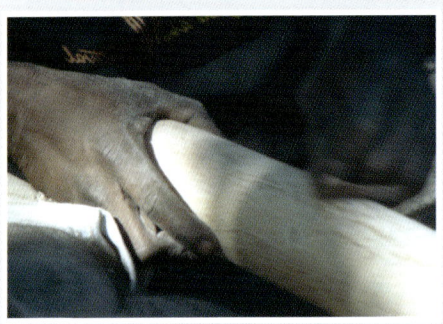

Sanding the blank in preparation for painting.

Ochre being ground on a hard surface and applied to a didjeridu.

Gundalk grass, a common reed, has been whittled and is used to apply fine ochre crosshatching.

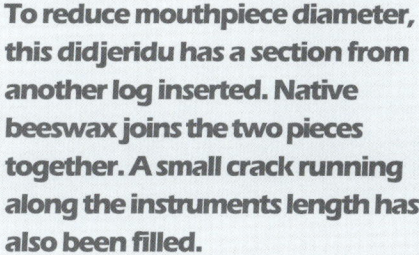

To reduce mouthpiece diameter, this didjeridu has a section from another log inserted. Native beeswax joins the two pieces together. A small crack running along the instruments length has also been filled.

The mouthpiece of this antique didjeridu was shaped with an axe and native beeswax was then applied. The surface of the didjeridu has been smeared with black and white ochre. It is much rougher than contemporary didjeridus as it has not been sanded.

The instrument on the left is decorated with Mimi spirits, while the one to the right has a crocodile.
Both are painted with ochre.

How to Play

When buying a didjeridu select one that is suitable for you. Often people buy inferior ones as souvenirs and later when they learn to play they are limited by the capabilities of the instrument. Make sure that you hear a demonstration of the instrument. Even though they may look similar, didjeridus vary dramatically in sound quality. The termites that hollowed the log did not take musical considerations into account while they were eating! If a retailer is unable to demonstrate a didjeridu for you, find another who can.

The length of a didjeridu determines its musical key. Long didjeridus are usually very deep in tone, short ones high. Both extremities-over two metres or under one are more difficult to play. Didjeridus 1.3-1.5 metres in length in the keys of C and D are ideal.

The mouthpiece of a didjeridu also needs to be the correct size. Select one with a diameter of approximately five centimetres. If it is too big it can be narrowed with wax. Often beginners choose ones with narrow mouthpieces, as they find them easier to play. As their playing matures and their lips and mouths strengthen, they find their instruments too small.

When starting, if you are trying to learn both circular breathing and sound creation, you are probably not doing either well. Learning circular breathing first is recommended.

The people of Kakadu and Western Arnhem Land believe that the ability to circular breathe and play the didjeridu is gained by consuming the eggs laid by a local frog species. For non-Aborigines learning these skills is a very different journey.

The most important thing to do when learning the didjeridu is to enjoy yourself. It's great fun, though depending on how you sound, it may not be for the neighbours! Learning can be very exciting, rewarding, and at times frustrating.

Playing the didjeridu consists of three main aspects — circular breathing, sound creation and rhythm. These can be learned with numerous techniques and exercises. The quest is a very personal one and like any instrument, some master it more easily than others.

These simple instructions can help you learn circular breathing and some sound creation techniques.

Circular breathing.

Didjeridu, saxophone and trumpet players all use circular breathing. The technique allows a continuous flow of air to be blown from the mouth. Once accomplished, it becomes second nature and can be done for long periods of time. It is the most difficult aspect of playing the didjeridu. Depending on the individual it can be learnt in hours, days or weeks. There are people who are keen to learn and never succeed. Don't become too frustrated or ill tempered when first learning. If you do, put the instrument down, have a break and think objectively about any mistakes you may be making and learn from them!

Physiologically the technique requires control of the lungs, diaphragm, mouth and tongue. However, the main task is cerebral — understanding sequence and coordinating muscles accordingly.

Didjeridu playing also involves inhaling through the nose and exhaling through the mouth. Breathing with the diaphragm allows larger more controlled breaths to be taken, and stronger exhalation. It requires moving the stomach out as you inhale and in when you exhale. We all breathe naturally in this way, however many people are taught to breathe with their rib cage only. Items like girdles make breathing with the diaphragm difficult.

Blowing a 'rasberry' into the didjeridu is the key to making sound. Pressing your lips against the mouthpiece creates backpressure, reducing the volume of air you exhale. Other narrower objects can be used to enhance this, making it easier to learn circular breathing. Short card board cylinders are ideal, as you can blow a raspberry into them and they are light and unobtrusive.

The key to circular breathing is to squeeze air from the mouth while snatching short breaths through the nose. Isolate the mouth from the throat and trachea by blocking its rear with the tongue. Puffing the cheeks allows more air to be contained in it. It is this air that makes circular breathing possible.

After the rear of the mouth has been blocked with the tongue, while maintaining a seal with the palette, the tongue is brought forward like a piston, forcing out as much air as possible. As air is expelled, a brief opportunity to inhale through the nose is created. With practise, slowly squeezing the air from the mouth can give several seconds with which to replenish the lungs.

It is best to prepare to circular breathe when the lungs are one third to half full. Exhaling fully does not leave enough air in to fill the mouth, making it impossible to take a breath.

When circular breathing is accomplished, many hours of enjoyment await, it is time to play the didjeridu. Initially there may be short pauses in airflow, accompanied by sound fluctuations. With practise these can be eradicated and a continuous drone created

The Breathing cycle.

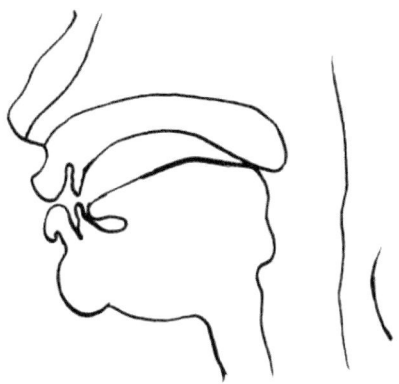

While 2/3 of the way through exhaling, the cheeks are filled with air. Blocking the rear of the mouth with the tongue and squeezing out the air, allows simultaneous inhalation through the nose.

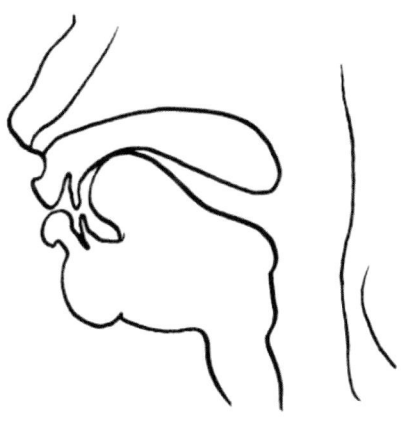

While inhaling, the tongue is brought forward like a piston. As the air in the mouth expires, inhalation is ceased and the tongue lowered to reopen the airway so air can be exhaled from the lungs. It is then returned to the rear of the mouth in preparation for the next cycle

Sound.

The various noises created on the didjeridu are made with the lips, tongue, throat and voice. Aboriginal people mimic a variety of birds, animals, ancestral beings and humans on the didjeridu. Any sound that can be made while vibrating the lips will be emitted from the didjeridu.

Before playing, didjeridus can be immersed or have water poured through their centre to improve sound quality and volume.

A good place to practise the didjeridu is in the bathroom. Most bathrooms have tile or cement floors that create excellent reverberation, making it easier to hear the instrument being played. Placing the end of a didjeridu in a bucket has a similar effect.

The main sound made by a didjeridu is its drone. The 'base' drone is created by blowing a 'raspberry' into it. It is important to press the lips firmly against the mouthpiece in order to create a proper seal. Moustaches and beards allow air to escape, making it more difficult to play.

Do not blow too hard and keep the lips flaccid. When the lips oscillate at the correct frequency the didjeridu will come to life, vibrating and making its characteristic sound. If the sound does not come, vary the intensity with which the lips are squeezed together and alter the pressure with which you blow.   Once you make the base drone start circular breathing. Try to keep the sound constant.

- The base drone can be varied by marginally increasing or decreasing the pressure with which you blow.
- Moving or flicking the tongue up and down in the mouth cavity creates an overtone of higher pitch.
- By bringing the tongue forward and quickly pressing it at the base of the upper front teeth in the way the letter 'd' is mouthed will create a bouncing or hopping sound like a kangaroo jumping.
- By tightly pursing the lips and giving a sharp puff makes a trumpeting sound. Skilled players are able to make several notes

- Rapidly and repeatedly pronouncing the letter 'k' while playing recreates the sound of the kookaburra or laughing jackass.
- Rolling 'r's or clearing the throat creates a rumbling sound.
- Using the tongue and voice at the same time creates double chords and overtones.

With regular practice, rhythms come naturally. Listening to music containing strong beats, including other didjeridu players can be very inspirational.

Initially your rhythms will be profoundly influenced by your breathing patterns. Your first rhythms will be the foundation for many others. As your technique improves your repertoire will increase dramatically.

Learning the didjeridu is a personal experience, and unless taught specific rhythms and songs, most people will develop their own individual way of playing.

Care

Being a hollow log, didjeridus are fairly robust. The most delicate features are their mouthpiece and decorative artwork. There are a number of things that can be done to care for the instrument.

- Do not leave didjeridus in direct sunlight for long periods of time. The heat will cause them to split. Cracks occur naturally over time, but can be filled with putty, glue or beeswax.
- When adding a mouthpiece do not use paraffin wax, use beeswax. The best way to add or enlarge a mouthpiece is to remove any existing wax from the didjeridu and then warm the wax you are going to apply until soft. Roll it and create a sausage, then press it onto the didjeridu. Make sure there are no air leaks. A good seal

can be created by using a lighter or match to melt a thin bead of wax around the outer lower edge of the mouthpiece. As the wax solidifies it will adhere to the wood.

- You can help preserve old didjeridus by taping plastic over one end and pouring half a cup of olive oil into the other and sealing it. Shake and rotate the instrument, then drain the oil. This rejuvenates the timber and enriches the sound.
- The artwork on didjeridus is susceptible to wear, particularly if the pigment is ochre. Immersing ochre painted didjeridus in water to improve their sound is not recommended as the agent bonding the ochre to the instrument is usually water soluble. If ochre is rubbing off, its bond can be strengthened by very carefully painting it with p.v.a. glue. Unlike other bonding agents, p.v.a. does not make white ochre transparent. It is however water-soluble, so don't wet it.
- As the length of a didjeridu determines its key, it can be changed by shortening the instrument. Sections that have been cut off cannot be reattached, so don't make any mistakes!
- A variety of didjeridu bags are available. Some are designed to carry several instruments. Bags that hold only one didj. are the most popular. The best ones are padded and have shoulder straps.

The didjeridu today

The didjeridu is no longer an unusual instrument used by Aborigines in northern Australia. It is now used throughout the world and features in ceremony, dance, rock bands, nightclubs and orchestras. The new-age movement uses the didjeridu for meditation and healing.

Now days, timber, bamboo, brass, glass, p.v.c., cardboard cylinders and vacuum cleaner nozzles are used to make didjeridus. They are decorated with acrylic paints and other materials, carved and burnt with an array of designs. A sliding two-piece didjeridu that changes key was developed by Charlie McMahon, further diversifying its performance capabilities.

The didjeridu brings pleasure to people of all ages.

Selected sources and further reading

Allen, J and Corris, P (eds), 1977:
The Journal of John Sweatman: A Nineteenth Century Surveying Voyage in North Australia & Torres Strait. (St Lucia: University of QLD Press.)

Bowden, John. 2000: Didjeridu. A complete guide to this ancient Aboriginal instrument. (Albany Creek, Queensland.)

Chaloupka, George. 1993: Journey in Time: the 50,000-year story of the Australian Aboriginal Rock Art of Arnhem Land. (J. B. Books, Marleston S.A.)

Dyer, Christine Adrian (Ed.). 1994: Kunwinjku Art From Injaluk 1991-1992 The John W.Kluge Commission. (U.S.A.)

Flood, Josephine. 1997: Rock Art Of the Dreamtime. (J.B. Books, Marleston S.A.)

Kaye, Peter. 1997: Play and enjoy the Didjeridu of the Australian Aboriginal. A newcomers guide. (Cairns, Queensland.)

Mountford, Charles P. December 1949: Exploring Stone Age Arnhem Land, in National Geographic Magazine. (National Geographic Society, Washington D.C.)

Moyle, Alice M. 1981: The Australian Didjeridu in World Archaeology Vol. 12.

Parker, Adrian. 1997: Images In Ochre. The Art and Craft of the Kunwinjku. (J.B. Books, Marleston S.A.)

Parker, Adrian and Roberts, David Andrew. 2003: Ancient Ochres. The Aboriginal Rock Paintings of Mount Borradaile. (J.B. Books, Marleston S.A.)

Simpson, Colin. 1951: Adam in Ochre. (Halstead Press, Sydney.)

Special thanks to Alex Nganjmirra, Chris Ngaboy, Leslie Ngaboy, Mark Nadjongorle, Joshua Bangar, Abel Naborhlborhl, Tony Bangalang, Jonathan Nadji and family, Mel, Ainslie, Sharon, Greg Miles, Environment Australia/Parks Australia North, Davidson's Arnhemland Safaris, Magela Cultural and Heritage Tours and the N.L.C.